From Darkness to Light
Author: Quvana Chambers
Published by: Hello Days of Grace, LLC
Englewood, Colorado, USA
Printer in USA
ISBN: 979-8-218-53366-3

Cover Design: Hello Days of Grace, LLC
Copyright © 2024 by Quvana Chambers. All rights reserved.

No part of this publication may be reproduced, distributed, or transmitted in any form or by any means, including photocopying, recording, or other electronic or mechanical methods, without the prior written permission of the author, except for brief quotations in a review. Unauthorized copying, scanning, or distribution is a violation of the author's intellectual property and constitutes theft. Thank you for your support of the author.

For permission requests, please contact:
Email: hello.daysofgrace@gmail.com

First Edition: December 2024

Dedication

This book is for God, my husband, my family, my friends, and for those who have gone before me—my parents, my brother, and my son.

Thank you, God my Father, for giving me the idea to do this and for helping me understand that all things are possible with You. You believed in me even when I didn't believe in myself, and You gave me the confidence to know that I can achieve this with You right here beside me! THANK YOU, JESUS!

Thank you all for your loving support.

Disclaimer

This book contains depictions of sensitive and potentially triggering topics, including but not limited to drug and alcohol use, sexual content, sexual assault, and death. Reader discretion is advised.

While the story is based on real-life events, the names of individuals and certain identifying details have been changed to protect their privacy and identity. Any similarities to persons, living or dead, beyond these changes, are coincidental. This work is intended to share a personal narrative and does not reflect the experiences or viewpoints of all individuals involved.

Part 1

In The Beginning

Chapter 1

"In the beginning God created the heavens and the earth. The earth was without form, and void; and darkness was on the face of the deep. And the Spirit of God was hovering over the face of the waters. Then God said, "Let there be light"; and there was light. God called the light Day, and the darkness He called Night. So the evening and the morning were the first day." Genesis 1:1-5

When I was about 13 years old, I watched a movie called "Thief in the Night," directed by Donald W. Thompson. It touched me and scared me into being careful about the choices I made. I didn't accept the Lord Jesus Christ and it wasn't something I fully understood either at that time, but looking back, I realize that a seed was planted in my heart that day.

A few years later, when I was 16, I spent time with my friend Cindy and her boyfriend, Fred. They invited me to a friend's apartment, and I was excited to go because it was a new experience for me. At the apartment, I met a guy I'll call John. I thought he was really cute, and the way he looked at me made me feel special.

After hanging out for a while, Cindy told me we were about to leave but promised we would come back. So, we went out to do some errands, and when we returned to John's place, Cindy plopped down on the couch, and I ended up meeting John's brother, who was just hanging out in the living room.

I think we were watching a movie, but the sound was so loud that John suggested we go to the bedroom so we could talk without having to shout. As we were headed to the bedroom, I got this strange pain in my chest. It was heavy like something bad was going to happen, but I comforted myself that nothing would happen to me because my friend was there.

We went into the bedroom and John locked the door. He sat me on the bed and began kissing me and slowly pushing me back. I was afraid and didn't know what to do. He started touching me in places I didn't want him to. I wanted to scream but I didn't and then I noticed that the TV began to get louder. I felt like I didn't know how to escape.

He was raping me.

I was trying to get away but I couldn't at that point. Then I just stopped trying and let him. Somehow, I got away. I didn't know how it happened. I bolted out of the bedroom and rushed through the main door of the apartment.

I paused to catch my breath, but John quickly caught up to me, so I took off running again. Just before I escaped, I heard him say, "I'm sorry," but I didn't stop. I found a spot to hide and peeked out, only to see that John's brother was also searching for me. They couldn't find me, so I left my hiding place and ran again.

I stopped when I spotted a cop talking to a woman. I was a wreck—my hair was a mess, my clothes were torn, and bruises marred my neck. Fear gripped me, and I hesitated to tell the cop what had happened. Instead, I asked if I could use his phone. He looked at me and said he didn't have one. He scrutinized me for a moment, then turned away to continue his conversation with the woman.

I wandered around until late into the night, feeling desperate to get home. I started knocking on random doors, hoping someone would help me. Finally, I came to a woman's door and knocked. When she opened it, I quickly apologized for bothering her so late and asked if I could use her phone. She agreed, but as I stepped inside, I could feel her eyes studying me.

I used the woman's phone to page Cindy to call me at that number. When Cindy called, I asked her to come get me. I found out she had left after I ran away. I reassured her that I was okay, but I admitted that something bad had happened. I didn't cry; I was just trying to hold it together. Cindy told me where she would pick me up, and then we hung up.

When I hung up the phone, the woman asked if I was okay. I told her yes, but she kept asking, her concern evident. I continued to reassure her, insisting that I was fine.

It hadn't hit me at that moment that I had been raped. Yes, I knew it happened, but I couldn't recognize that. I was just trying to hold it together and not cry, but the woman could sense that something was wrong. I thanked her, and I think she wanted to hug me, but I honestly can't remember if we did or not.

As I walked out of her apartment, I spotted Cindy and Fred's car and hurried to get inside. Relief washed over me when I settled into the car with Cindy. That's when I finally started to tell her what had happened, and the tears began to pour out. Both Cindy and Fred were furious.

Fred drove to John's apartment building and then Cindy jumped out of the car with Fred and rushed into John's apartment. She found the guy who hurt me, and she was so angry that she hit him so hard she broke his jaw. Fred went after John's brother and ended up cutting him with a knife. They called the cops, but my friend told me not to say anything because if I did, the police would deport Fred.

After the chaos settled, they took me to Cindy's mom's house, where we recounted everything. Her sadness was palpable, but so was her anger. Afterward, Cindy drove me home, and I felt a mix of relief and fear about everything that had just happened.

I was terrified to tell my family what had happened, but eventually, I mustered the courage to let my mom know. She was furious and wanted to confront Cindy, but I stopped her. I knew that would only make things worse. A few days passed, and by then, I had shared my story with the rest of my family. They all encouraged me to report the incident to the police, but fear gripped me, and I left home to go to my neighbor's house across the street. I spent time hanging out on their back patio, just sitting there in silence. I didn't want to go to the police; too many days had already gone by, and I doubted they would believe me.

After some time spent wrestling with my thoughts, I decided to report the incident. When I finally made that decision, the female officer who was working with me said I would need to return to take a lie detector test. Hearing that made me feel terrible, as if they didn't believe me. The officer mentioned there were parts of my story that didn't add up, which only deepened my feelings of doubt and shame. After that, I felt even worse and ultimately decided not to go back.

In the following months, I mostly spent time with Cindy and Fred. I didn't date anyone because I was terrified of reliving that traumatic experience, so I kept my distance from men. One day, while we were out, I met one of their friends, who went by the name Ponytail in Spanish. I was nervous to meet him, but he turned out to be quite nice.

Ponytail and I ended up dating for about a month, and one day, the four of us ended up partying together at Cindy's apartment. That party opened the floodgates to more nights of partying, drinking, and smoking weed, though I didn't smoke as much weed as I drank alcohol.

While partying, Ponytail hinted that he wanted to have sex with me. I was filled with fear as memories of the past and being forced into a sexual situation flooded my mind, so I did what I thought would be protecting myself. I had sex with him. That one time of sexual intercourse was the only experience I had had with sex so I thought if I willingly had sex with him, then I wouldn't get raped again. It didn't stop me from being petrified. Ponytail wasn't forceful but I still hadn't wanted to have sex.

After that, Ponytail and I split and I started partying and having more sex with other men.

Chapter 2

At 18 years old, I was still partying a lot, and it was only leading me deeper into a dark place. Despite the partying, I started working at Mr. Goodcents. I never got the chance to finish high school—I only needed two more credits to graduate. A good friend of mine told me about Job Corps, which would allow me to finish those credits while learning new skills, so I decided to give it a shot.

I ended up discovering a real passion for welding and trained in that trade while working on my diploma. I spent about a year and three months there and met some amazing people. When I completed the program, I returned home with $1,500 in my pocket and started looking for a job as a welder. Unfortunately, I didn't land one, and I felt like society just wasn't ready to accept a female welder yet.

Feeling defeated, I fell back into drinking and partying. Then my sister got a job as a housekeeper at a hospital, so I followed her lead and started working there too. About nine months later, I managed to buy my first car from the junkyard.

That summer, I found an opportunity to work with kids, which turned out to be cool and fun. The kids were a challenge, but I was learning a lot from them. After spending the day with the kids, I would go back to my job as a housekeeper at a daycare. Even during all this, I was still seeking every chance I could find to party and drink. I was extremely depressed, but I had become good at hiding it. Work became my way of coping with the tough times, providing a distraction from everything I was feeling.

One day, a woman started working at the daycare whom I'll call Angel. She truly lived up to her name. It felt like she came into my life as a guiding light, helping me find my way back to where I was meant to be.

At that time, I was already 24 years old. Angel was kind and friendly, but I noticed something different about her. I couldn't quite put my finger on it, but her warmth and kindness drew me in.

She would engage me in deep conversations, and I genuinely enjoyed her friendship. One day, she opened up about some mistakes she had made as a Christian, and it impressed me. Even though she didn't know me well, she allowed me to see that through her story and experiences, God still loved her. She shared how Jesus had forgiven her for her mistakes. I can't share the details of her journey, but hearing her story helped me remember that God can love and forgive us, even through our sins.

One night, I called my friend to go out partying. By the end of the night, we ended up back at her place, both of us completely drunk, and we ended up messing around with each other. When that happened, I felt utterly confused and hit an all-time low.

The next morning, I got up to go to work and immediately started looking for Angel as soon as I arrived. I wanted to tell her that I was ready to give my life to Jesus. My coworkers informed me that Angel hadn't arrived yet, so I let them know I was searching for her. I tried to focus on cleaning my rooms, but my mind was still distracted and confused, constantly thinking about how much I wanted to talk to her.

Just as I came out of the room I was cleaning, I saw Angel there. Without hesitation, I told her I wanted to give my life to Jesus. Her face lit up with happiness, and she pulled me into a closet, excited to pray with me. She had me repeat after her as we prayed for forgiveness and repentance for my sins, asking Jesus to come into my heart. At first, I didn't feel anything in my heart, but as soon as that thought crossed my mind, the feeling of love rushed into me and God's love washed over me and filled my heart. I felt an overwhelming sense of love.

I hugged Angel tightly and thanked her profusely. As we exited the closet, we ran into my friend Ted, the maintenance guy. All I wanted to do was hug him. He looked at me with concern and asked if I was okay. I smiled and said yes. Then I hugged a woman I didn't particularly like, and surprisingly, I felt so much love for her. I went on to hug another woman I didn't care for, and she looked at me like I was crazy, asking if I was okay. I simply replied that I was fine. I felt incredible.

Angel invited me to her church, and as I thought about it, I worried it might be too far for me to attend. Even though I had given my life to Christ, I hadn't yet let go of my partying lifestyle.

Chapter 3

I continued sleeping around and partying. During that time, I met a man at a club, and our relationship was purely physical; we would only meet up to have sex—nothing more, nothing less. One day, he jokingly mentioned that he wanted to get me pregnant, but I quickly told him I didn't want to have a baby with him since we didn't love each other.

That night, as I lay in bed staring up at the ceiling, I couldn't shake the feeling that this wasn't how I wanted my life to be. I realized I couldn't keep living like this. My life had to change.

A month later, I noticed that my period was late. I decided to buy a pregnancy test, and when I took it, the result came back blank. That night, while babysitting my niece, she laid her head on my stomach, and I felt a strange pressure and pain on my left side that I couldn't quite understand. Then it hit me.

I was pregnant.

I went back to the trash can to retrieve the pregnancy test, and sure enough, the previously blank test now read "pregnant." It sounds strange, but that's actually how I discovered I was expecting. After being in total shock, I managed to pull myself together and went to a clinic the next day to confirm the results. When they tested me, the staff came into the room and congratulated me on my very unexpected pregnancy.

Instead of feeling joy, I freaked out. It was far from a celebratory moment for me. The woman at the clinic apologized and asked if I needed to discuss other options. I knew she was referring to whether I was considering terminating the pregnancy. A wave of sadness washed over me, and I felt a deep sense of disappointment in myself. Here I was, barely able to take care of myself, let alone another human being, a child. I won't lie, though—I seriously considered the abortion.

I continued to deliberate about the possibility of caring for this child. The only person I could confide in was my best friend. When I opened up to her about my feelings and thoughts, she urged me not to go through with it, sharing that she had faced a similar situation with her own child and deeply regretted her decision. She didn't want me to experience the pain and guilt she had lived with ever since.

I truly valued her perspective and took her words to heart. After carefully considering what she had said, I decided against getting an abortion. The moment I made that decision, it felt like a heavy burden had been lifted from my shoulders. All I felt was true peace and joy, along with an overwhelming sense of love, knowing that I would have my child.

As time went on, I continued working, but the doctors put me on light duty with restrictions against heavy lifting due to early pregnancy spotting. Thankfully, the spotting eventually went away. My main job at the time was at the daycare. One day, a parent came to drop off her child, and after a few conversations, we naturally became friends.

I discovered through our talks that she was an OBGYN. When she learned I was pregnant, she offered to be my doctor, and I readily agreed. She was an amazing doctor and took excellent care of me throughout my pregnancy.

One day, while I was at home, I suddenly started feeling pain. At that moment, I had no idea it was labor pains. I asked my niece if she could take me to the hospital, and she started getting ready. However, as she was preparing, I felt like she was taking forever. My impatience got the better of me, and I decided to drive myself.

It was a crazy decision because I had to pull over multiple times due to the pain. By the time I finally reached the hospital, my niece had beaten me there. She was waiting for me, looking concerned and wondering why I had left without her.

The hospital staff wheeled me into a room, which I think was either the ICU or labor and delivery. At that moment, I didn't know what to think. They ran tests and placed a monitoring machine on me to check how my baby boy was doing. I had learned at six weeks that he had a heartbeat—and a strong one at that. Later, I found out the gender, and when I discovered he was a boy, I felt a wave of happiness because I had wanted a son. I decided to name him Quinton, which means "strong."

Then, my doctor entered the room. When I looked at her face, I saw tears welling up in her eyes. She explained that my son was having a hard time and that we needed to perform a c-section. She told me that if I attempted a vaginal birth, he wouldn't make it. Looking deeply into my eyes, she said it was a 50/50 chance with the c-section. I silently agreed, understanding the gravity of the situation. My doctor was so compassionate and kind, reassuring me that everything would be okay. She left the room to let the nurses prepare me for surgery.

The nurses explained that they would be giving me an epidural. They told me it would involve a needle going into my lower spinal cord, and a medicine would numb me from the waist down. Once they administered the epidural, they laid me back on the table.

I later found out that my sister had been in the surgery room with me, but in that moment, all I could focus on was lying there, numb from the waist down. I could feel the doctor tugging a bit, but I was completely in and out of consciousness the entire time. I had no sense of how long we had been in there.

Finally, I saw my son in the incubator. My sister told me that the doctor had placed him by my side after they got him out, but I had no memory of that moment. He looked so small in the incubator, and his tiny hands were just precious.

When I closed my eyes, the hospital transported my son to Children's Mercy Hospital. Lying in my hospital bed, I couldn't shake the worry about him being all alone. I truly believe God heard my silent prayers because, unbeknownst to me, it was on my mom's heart to be with him.

At that time, she was really sick, but my sister drove her to Children's Mercy, where my mom stayed by my son's side the whole time. The nurses there took excellent care of her.

I didn't know it then, but God had already orchestrated everything, answering my prayers before I even voiced them. This all unfolded into the next day, May 19, 2003. My doctor and friend came to see me, visibly emotional and crying. I was so grateful she was there. She told me she was going to give me a pass to go see my son, which brought me immense relief. I thanked her and expressed how glad I was that we had become friends. She was not just an amazing doctor; she was also a true friend.

She left the room, and I called my niece to bring me some clothes so I could get ready to see my son. I was in pain from the surgery, but the thought of being with him gave me the strength to move despite the discomfort. I needed him to know I was there for him.

As I lay in bed waiting for my niece to arrive at the hospital, I received a phone call from Children's Mercy. They delivered the devastating news that my son was bleeding in his brain and that there was nothing more they could do. They didn't know how much longer he had and urged me to get there as soon as possible to see him. He had been on life support. All I could manage to say was "okay" before I hung up the phone, feeling my heart sink.

To be honest, I didn't fully understand what the doctor had said. It felt like my mind was stuck in a fog, and the news didn't sink in until I saw my niece arrive with my clothes and her baby. I told her what had happened and what the doctor had said, and that's when I became hysterical.

I cried so hard, realizing the gravity of the situation—I was going to lose my son. My one-year-old niece noticed my reaction and wrapped her tiny arms around me, giving me the biggest hug. It was tight, and she wouldn't let go. At that moment, it felt like God Himself was using my little niece to comfort me, wrapping me in love.

I cried hard. Endlessly.

My eldest niece, Latasha, handed me my clothes to change into, and I was grateful she had brought her little daughter along; I honestly don't know if I would have made it through those agonizing moments without them. My life felt shattered.

When my aunt arrived to drive us to Children's Mercy, the three of us set off together. I was in so much pain, both physically and emotionally, and I continued to weep until we reached the hospital. My aunt spoke to me during the drive, but I couldn't hear her over my thoughts and feelings. I'm sure she was talking about God, though, because she loved Him deeply, and her faith was a constant source of strength.

When we arrived at the hospital, I got out of the car and we entered the elevator. I continued to cry out to the Lord, begging Him to save my son. There was a man in the elevator with us who looked completely nervous and uncomfortable, but in that moment, I didn't care about anything else. All I felt was the overwhelming pain of losing my son. I was screaming until we reached my son's floor, and then I finally managed to calm down enough to get off the elevator and walk to the NICU.

When I saw him hooked up to the life support machine, he looked so sweet and small. He wasn't fully developed, so his skin and limbs had a slight reddish hue, but he was still perfect—my son, Quinton Lee. I was happy to have him with me. In that moment, my thoughts were that he was fine, and I didn't need to make any decisions about taking him off life support at all.

But just as I thought that, the machine alarmed, and the nurses rushed in, saying that if we didn't make a decision now, my son would make one for us. We prayed together, and at that moment, I didn't know I didn't need to get him baptized, but I understood he had been dedicated to God. I knew God would take care of him, and that he belonged to our Father.

I continued to cry in despair, and my family took me into a separate room to wait for the staff to bring my son to me. While I waited, my aunt prayed and read scripture for me. Finally, the hospital staff brought me my son. I held him in my hands; he was so tiny, fitting perfectly in the palm of my hand. His head reached the tips of my fingers, while his body lay cradled in my palm.

In that moment, he felt so alive in my hands.

I looked at my son through my tears, and to me, it just looked like he was sleeping. But after a while, I realized he was no longer alive. I called the doctors in to check for signs of life, and they confirmed what I already knew: my son was gone, even though he was right there in the palm of my hands. My heart was shattered knowing he was no longer with me. Could any amount of crying truly capture how I felt? In the beginning, I couldn't even think about it.

I had wanted to abort him because I didn't think I could take care of him, but my friend changed my mind. I tried to keep him, and I was determined to be a good mom. But in those moments when I cried out to God to save my son, I realized that was exactly what He had done. God had brought my son home to Him because my son had served his purpose here on Earth. I love my son deeply, but I am so grateful that God took him there, where there's no better place for him to be.

When I look back on my life, I can see how God reached down from heaven into the darkness of my existence. Just like it says in Acts 26:18, "to open their eyes, in order to turn them from darkness to light, and from the power of Satan to God, that they may receive forgiveness of sins and an inheritance among those who are sanctified by faith in Me." He truly brought me from darkness into His light. The Lord Jesus had always been there for me, even when I was unaware of His presence. It's incredible to think about how He guided me through my struggles, leading me toward hope and healing.

I sat there in that little room, crying more and more. The nurse came to take my son because I knew it was time to let him go. I was filled with sadness and heartbreak. My auntie took me back to the hospital where I had delivered, and I just laid there on the bed, feeling completely depressed—mourning, grieving. Yet, amid all those feelings, I also felt a sense of strength. I didn't know where it came from, nor could I understand it.

The next day, I began calling around to look for a funeral home. I asked the nurses how long they would keep my son's body at the hospital because I knew it would be financially tough. They told me I had up to a year. I wasn't sure how long it would take for me to gather the funds, so I needed just a little more time. It also gave me something to focus on during my grieving process.

I called one funeral home and explained my situation. They were compassionate and understanding. They suggested I visit the government assistance welfare office downtown to see if I could get financial help. So, the next day, when the hospital released me, I went downtown to the welfare office to see if I could get help paying for my baby's funeral. The cost of the funeral home would be $1,000, but the government office could only assist me with $255. I took that, pooled it with my own $500, and went to the funeral home to pay for the service with a check. Now, I only had $245 left to pay.

After visiting the funeral home, I went with a friend to look for clothes for my son. She was not going to be there for the funeral service, which is why she joined me. After buying the clothes, we returned to the funeral home. As we rode down the elevator, we encountered a man who worked there. He took us down to the basement, where we saw my son. My friend said her goodbyes, and we cried together before making our way back up to the main floor.

The man was with us, and I asked if he had ever seen anyone visit their loved ones so often. He looked at me with such a serious face and said no, that I was the first one. For some reason, I found that to be the most hilarious thing I had ever heard, especially the way he looked when he said it. I needed that laugh because, while I was down in the basement, my thoughts had turned dark. I had considered taking my son and just running away with him. I wanted to take him home because I loved him so much, but I quickly snapped out of that mindset, knowing it was better to lay him to rest.

Then, I started thinking about who could officiate my baby's funeral, and a church came to mind: Praise Chapel. I had only been there once to watch a play.

I looked up Praise Chapel's phone number and gave them a call. A woman named Dawn answered and asked how she could help me. When she heard my story, she was sympathetic and empathetic. She shared that she had lost a child too, which made her understanding even more profound.

Dawn listened to me, and in that moment, I felt a sense of peace. She seemed like a truly warm person, and her kindness touched my heart. I needed that kind of love during such a difficult time, and God had blessed me with it. Before we ended the call, she invited me to the church on Sunday. I told her I would go because I needed a place to worship anyway.

When I went to the church that Sunday, I walked in feeling nervous and a little scared because I didn't know what to expect. Once I stepped inside, I found a seat and settled in. Slowly, I began to feel more welcomed by the people around me. Everyone was caring, and I didn't feel out of place at all.

When the worship started, I watched as people sang and lifted their hands. I don't think I lifted my hands in worship at that time, and I can't even remember what the pastor was preaching about. I just remember him asking us to raise our hands if we wanted to give our lives to Jesus. My hand shot up so quickly. Then he invited me to come down to the altar so he could pray for me.

I walked down the long aisle, hearing the sound of people clapping and feeling their excitement. It felt like that walk down the aisle took forever.

I felt ashamed and loved all at the same time. As I began to cry, I suddenly felt someone come up behind me.

The pastor thanked me for coming down and then asked the crowd if anyone else wanted to give their life to Jesus. The person behind me began to pray over me, and I became even more emotional. I felt touched by God, as if I was finally home. It was amazing how good God is.

The next day was my son's funeral service. When I saw him, he was dressed in his baptism outfit, and he looked absolutely adorable. I was there with my mom, dad, and a friend, and I couldn't help but cry when I saw him lying there. He looked like he was just sleeping. I felt the funeral home had done a wonderful job.

After the service, we got into our cars to follow the procession to the burial grounds. All my family was there, along with a few people from my job. The night before the service, I had written a poem for my son, and before the burial, I read it aloud. Pastor Steve spoke a beautiful and powerful message and then asked if anyone wanted to receive Jesus as their Lord and Savior. I saw a few hands go up, and he prayed for them.

It was a beautiful experience—watching the entire process unfold and witnessing God move in the hearts of those people.

This is just a small portion of my testimony and how Jesus saved me.

Part 2

Life of Being Saved

Chapter 4

As time went on, my relationship with God began to blossom. I started reading His Word, and it truly spoke to me. One particular memory that stands out is when I was reading about Jacob and Esau. Their story resonated with me in relation to my relationship with my older brother. We didn't have a great relationship, but I could see that God had a plan for him, especially since he was getting married soon.

For some reason, I didn't want to go to his wedding. I made the excuse that I was busy with church activities, but the truth was, I simply didn't want to be there. I still hadn't truly forgiven him. When my family went to Florida for the wedding, even my mom, who was very ill at that time, attended. My brother had even gone so far as to arrange dialysis treatment for her down there so she could be present.

My aunt told me they had a great time and mentioned that I should have gone. Hearing that made me feel guilty, and I instantly regretted my decision not to attend. As I continued reading about Jacob and Esau, I felt God moving on my heart, urging me to reach out to my brother.

By a miracle, my friend and I had planned a vacation to New York for my birthday, but we ultimately decided not to go. I had booked a round-trip flight for myself for $147.89, but since we couldn't make the trip, I had to cancel my flight.

In Genesis 32:22-24, Jacob prepares to meet his brother Esau after years of separation. He is anxious and fearful of Esau's reaction, remembering how he had deceived him in the past. That night, Jacob wrestles with a mysterious man until daybreak, refusing to let go until he receives a blessing. This encounter leaves Jacob with a new name, Israel, signifying his struggle with God and man.

In Genesis 33:1-11, Jacob approaches Esau, who comes to meet him with 400 men. To Jacob's surprise, Esau runs to him and embraces him, showing forgiveness and love. They reconcile, and Jacob offers gifts to Esau, acknowledging his past wrongs. Esau graciously accepts, and they share a moment of peace, reaffirming their brotherly bond.

During that time, I envisioned myself and my older brother apologizing to each other. It felt like a healing moment, where the weight of the past was lifted, and we could finally move forward with understanding and love.

I wanted to make things right between us, so I decided to use my canceled flight money to book a flight to Florida instead. In the end, I only spent an additional $7.39 out of my own pocket.

I let my brother know that I would be flying to Florida to spend a week with him and his wife. I saved up money for the trip because my heart's desire was to spoil him, just like Jacob did for Esau. Before boarding the plane, I was reading a book my pastor had written about his life with Christ and how Jesus transformed him.

As I was reading, I noticed a lady who sat next to me in an open seat, but I wasn't in the mood to talk to anyone, so I buried my head in my book and kept reading. When they called for passengers to board, I gathered my things and boarded the plane. I settled into my seat, buckled my seatbelt, and picked up my book again. I glanced up briefly to see how many more people were boarding, trying to gauge how much longer we would be waiting.

That's when I noticed the lady again. It turned out that she was sitting in the aisle seat of my row, right across from me. She didn't have a carry-on and smiled as she settled in. I felt a gentle prompting from God to engage with her, but I really wasn't trying to talk to anyone. However, when she said hi, I felt compelled to respond.

I tried to get back into my book, but she asked me where I was headed. I told her I was going to Florida to see my brother and his wife. She remarked that it was nice of me to do that, so I finally put my book down and asked her about her destination. That's when she shared that she was going to see her dying mother, and my heart sank. I sympathized with her because, not long after my brother's wedding, my mother had passed away too.

I felt heartbroken for this lady, and I genuinely listened to her as she spoke. She needed someone to hear her, and I prayed that she would make it in time to say goodbye to her mother. Thank God He allowed me to focus and listen to this woman who needed someone. I prayed for her silently, but only God knows if she made it in time. I truly hoped so.

When the plane landed, I said goodbye to her and headed to retrieve my suitcase.

My oldest brother was there to pick me up, and I was thrilled to see him. I embraced him in a warm hug, feeling grateful to be together. We headed to his car, and he drove us to his home, which was quite a distance from the airport. We had a lot to catch up on, and I expressed my apologies for missing his wedding. He told me it was fine, but I could tell he was genuinely hurt by my absence.

When we arrived at his house, I thought it looked pretty small from the outside, but once we stepped inside, I was surprised by how spacious it was. He asked me to put my suitcase in the living room, and that's when I met his wife. She was incredibly kind and sweet. I also met his daughter, who was about one or two years old, though I can't quite remember her exact age. She had beautiful red hair, sparkling blue eyes, and a smile that lit up the room.

My brother showed me around the Tampa area, and he had planned out fun activities for each day I was there. One of those days, we went to see the movie "Avatar," and it was crazy good. We had a fantastic time together. One night, while my brother and I were talking, he mentioned that I should be careful about what I told my sister-in-law regarding myself because she had told him she really liked me. I appreciated how well she treated me, and I knew that my brother sharing this was his way of apologizing for the past. God is so good.

We also looked at wedding photos from their special day, and it was beautiful to see my mom in those pictures. It warmed my heart to witness how happy she was.

The next day was my last in Florida, and I asked my brother to take us to his favorite restaurant. He took me to a great place, and we enjoyed a delicious meal together. Wanting to bless my brother, I paid for everyone's meal that night. He jokingly asked if I was a "baller," but what he didn't know was that I had saved up money and had also been paid that day, which allowed me to cover the costs.

I want to thank my Lord and Savior, Jesus Christ, for putting it on my heart to make things right with my brother. Only Jesus could facilitate that reconciliation and bring peace between us. Later, I learned that the restaurant my brother chose wasn't actually his favorite, but he was considerate and thoughtful about my finances, so he picked a different place. Regardless, I wanted to show him how much I loved him and how deeply I wanted to apologize for missing his wedding.

God had great plans in allowing me to visit Florida because, after a few years, my older brother passed away.

I had worried that maybe he hadn't made it to heaven, but the Father confirmed that he had. During my visit, my brother had been deeply touched and opened his heart to God, accepting Jesus.

My brother passed away peacefully in his sleep at the hospital.

Chapter 5

As time went on, I started to grow weary in my heart. I was rarely reading the Word of God or applying it to my life. I began to have negative thoughts about my Bible study leaders. My mom was sick, and my family and I took care of her, which meant I wasn't in church as much as I used to be.

I decided it was time to sit myself down because I wasn't being completely honest with myself or others, but I struggled to communicate my feelings effectively. I felt it was best to step back from all the activities I was involved in at church, except for cleaning. It was a necessary break to reflect and regain my focus on my relationship with God.

During this time, I felt down and depressed. My mom wanted me to read the Bible to her, but I didn't really feel like it. Truthfully, I was so messed up that I didn't feel worthy to read God's Word, yet I did it anyway. I read the book of Matthew to her, and God touched me through His Word. I began to cry, and my mom noticed, asking me what was wrong.

I asked her to pray for me, and she hesitated, saying she didn't know how to pray like I did. I reassured her that God would hear her no matter what. When she prayed for me, I felt God touch me again through her simple words. It was a beautiful and powerful moment. While nothing immediately changed, I felt a sense of relief wash over me.

I took on the responsibility of caring for my mom. One night, around 10 PM, she mentioned feeling pain in her chest. I asked if she wanted me to call an ambulance, but all she said was no, just to pray for her. So I did.

She said she felt a little better, so I got ready for bed. Almost an hour later, she woke me up, telling me it was hot and asking me to turn up the air conditioner. I got up and adjusted it for her, then gave her a cold compress to put on her head. I asked if she felt better, and she said yes, so I went back to sleep.

However, she woke me again, saying she felt like she was going to throw up. I quickly got her something to throw up in, but she was so restless, and I didn't understand what was happening with her. Around 4 AM, I decided to call my niece to see if she could come over and stay with my mom so I could go to work. Before my niece got to the house, my mom had asked me for water, but I was so exhausted that I didn't get up. She asked me a couple of times if I could get her water, but I still didn't respond.

When my niece walked in at 6 AM, I asked her to get a cold glass of water for my mom. She did, and I finally mustered the energy to get ready for work. But when my niece called out to my mom, there was no response. I looked over at her and quickly told my niece to call 911 because I knew something was seriously wrong. My mom was unresponsive.

Thankfully, the ambulance arrived quickly. They asked us what had happened, and we explained the situation. They began performing CPR on my mom. As they lifted her onto the gurney and carried her to the ambulance, they asked if I wanted them to continue CPR, and I said yes. I couldn't understand why they even needed to ask me that. My niece rode with them, while I hopped into my car and followed them to the closest hospital.

When I arrived at the hospital, they already had my mom in the ER. I made my way to the waiting room, and a man approached me to ask if I wanted them to proceed with CPR. I said yes again. By that time, it had already been 30 minutes.

The man returned, and I discovered he was the chaplain. After 45 minutes, he told me that the doctor didn't think there was anything else they could do if she didn't come back soon, and that she would likely be brain dead. I looked at the man and screamed at God. I cried out that I didn't want her to go, that I wanted her to stay with me. I took it very hard, and anger washed over me. I didn't even realize I was feeling angry, but I was upset with God and with all of His people.

Chapter 6

After everything that happened, I felt really lonely so I decided to give online dating a try. I started talking to this guy, and when we met in person, we ended up sleeping together. I felt completely empty afterward. I thought maybe it was just a one-time mistake, but then I met another guy. We went on a couple of dates, and again, we ended up in bed. This pattern repeated a few more times. Each time, I felt worse about myself, like I was losing my worth, piece by piece. These relationships didn't bring me any joy or fulfillment—just a deepening sense of depression.

Then, one day, I got a message from a man named Don. It was simple—just a winky face through the dating app—but something about it caught my attention. We started chatting, and eventually exchanged phone numbers. I was immediately drawn to him. His voice was deep and confident, the kind that makes you feel safe just listening to it. We talked on the phone for weeks, maybe two or three, before we finally sent each other pictures. He was handsome, and he thought I was beautiful too.

We kept talking for two months, and eventually, Don asked if we could meet in person. I hesitated, telling him I wanted to get to know him more over the phone. The truth was, I didn't want to make the same mistake again. I didn't want to rush into anything and end up feeling even more lost. I wanted something real, something that connected us on a deeper level. So, we talked—just talked—for two whole years.

It wasn't that I hadn't had opportunities to meet other people during that time. For years, while I was serving in the church, I had committed to staying celibate, focusing on God and my spiritual growth. But when I began to drift away from church and let myself slip from God's presence, I slowly fell back into my old patterns. That's why talking to Don felt like a blessing. He helped me stay centered, even while I was struggling to rediscover myself.

Even though I had been looking for someone local, the fact that Don lived in a different state ended up being a good thing. It gave me the space I needed to truly get to know him without the pressure of physical intimacy getting in the way. There was no rushing into anything, no chance of falling back into the same old mistakes. It allowed us to build something real, something deeper, and for that, I was grateful.

After two years of talking, I finally flew out to Denver, Colorado to meet Don. We had an amazing time together. I felt so comfortable, like I had known him forever. During that visit, we made love. But soon, the time came for me to head back home, Don took me to the airport. I got upset with him because I wanted him to come inside and wait with me, but he explained that if he left the car parked out front for too long, he could get a ticket. I should've understood that from the start, but in the moment, my emotions got the best of me. He called me before I boarded the plane, and after talking it over, I understood where he was coming from.

On the flight back, I found myself thinking about moving to Denver. I figured I'd give it six months, but in reality, it took me a year to pay off all my debt. I didn't want anything holding me back or tying me financially to Kansas City. I gave my job a three-month notice to give them time to find someone to replace me. My administrator really wanted me to stay and even tried to talk to Don when he came to Kansas City to drive me back to Denver with my car.

Before I left, my coworkers threw me a going-away party. It meant so much to me. I had never had anyone do something like that for me before, and it made me feel so special and appreciated. Don was over the moon. He was so happy for me and proud that they had celebrated me like that. It made him feel proud that they showed how much they cared about me. The whole experience was a mix of emotions—excitement, nervousness, and a deep sense of being valued.

We left for Denver on August 14th, 2013. Don drove the car, packed with everything I owned, and we made the eight-hour drive from Kansas City to Denver. When we crossed into Colorado, we pulled over and took a picture by the state sign—it felt like the start of a new chapter.

We drove into the city and checked into a hotel for the night, but I didn't like it because the whole place smelled like cigarettes.

The next day, we started looking for a more permanent place to stay, but after hours of searching, we couldn't find anything. Frustrated, I ended up booking another hotel, this time for a full week. Each day, we continued our search, but nothing seemed to work out. I started to feel scared and overwhelmed. I had a job lined up before we left, and when I went in for the interview, everything seemed to go well. But after days of waiting for a call back, I heard nothing. When I finally reached out, the woman who interviewed me told me they had given the position to someone else.

I was devastated. I had been counting on that job, and now, I didn't know what to do. I went back to the hotel and cried out to God, praying for Him to help us find a place to live and for a new job opportunity. I felt so lost in that moment, like everything was falling apart.

Then, on the very last day of our hotel stay, a Friday, the Lord blessed us with a place to live. I was beyond grateful—Thank you, Lord Jesus. Thank you, God. It was a reminder that even in the most uncertain moments, He was there, guiding us and making a way when it seemed impossible.

As we were on our way to pick up the keys for our new place, Don was driving, and out of nowhere, we got pulled over. My car only had one license plate, but in Colorado, two were required. I didn't even know that at the time. We were actually on our way to Don's niece and nephew's house when it happened. To make matters worse, Don had a warrant for his arrest for something that had happened in the past, involving an incident with his brother while he was trying to protect his mom—or at least that's what he had explained to me. The officer had no choice but to take him to jail.

I was terrified. I had no idea how to navigate the city on my own yet. Thankfully, we were close to his nephew's house, so I stayed there for the night. The next day, I had to figure out how to get down to the jail to bail Don out. I called Don's mom to get some advice—she told me not to bail him out. She said Don was tough and could handle being in jail for a short while, and she was sure they would dismiss the charge with time served. After thinking about it, I took her advice, and I'm glad I did. It saved me a lot of money—money I really couldn't afford to lose. I only had $400 left until my next paycheck the following week.

When Don was released, I picked him up after work, and we finally went to get the keys to our new apartment. It was such a relief to step into our place for the first time. After getting all of our things out of storage and moving in, we started to settle down. We didn't have any furniture at the time, so Don got creative and made us a bed out of bags of clothing. But I still needed a job.

Don's nephew suggested a few places to try, so I started making calls. One place I contacted told me they had openings and asked if I could come down immediately to fill out an application. I didn't hesitate. I went straight there, and they ended up interviewing me on the spot. Before I could even finish filling out the paperwork, they told me I was hired.

Thank you, God. Within three weeks of moving from Kansas City to Denver, I had a place to live and a job. It felt like such a blessing—God had heard my prayers. I ended up working at that job for a year. Looking back, I'm just so thankful for how everything worked out, even when it all seemed uncertain at first.

Chapter 7

One day, as I was reflecting on the way we had been living, it really hit me—we weren't married yet, and I began to feel convicted about it. It weighed heavily on my heart, so I talked to Don and told him that I wanted to stop having sex until we were married. To my surprise, he said he felt the same way.

In that moment, we both realized that we wanted to realign our lives with our faith. We repented, asking God for forgiveness, and we made a promise to each other and to God that we would abstain from sex until we were married. It wasn't an easy decision, but we knew it was the right one for us. It brought a sense of peace and a renewed purpose to our relationship, like we were finally on the right path.

After deciding to abstain from sex until we were married, Don and I began thinking about when we wanted to tie the knot. We thought June would be perfect because that was the month we first started talking on the phone. Once we settled on the date, I started planning our wedding. I was determined to make it special, even with our limited budget. I went to Dollar Tree and bought supplies to make our centerpieces by hand. Don's mom helped out by arranging for Don's sister to make our cake, and she also told us about an affordable venue where we could hold the ceremony.

We called around to a few churches to see if they could officiate our wedding, but they all wanted to charge more than we could afford. That's when we asked Don's nephew if he would be willing to officiate our wedding. He went the extra mile and got himself ordained with an online course just so he could marry us. We were so grateful for that—it truly felt like a gift.

When it came time to look for a wedding dress, Don's baby sister took me to a Hispanic boutique that sold beautiful dresses. I found one that I loved, originally priced at $180. The lady working there must have seen how much I wanted it because she told me she'd give it to me for $120. But the truth was, I only had $60 on me. That's when Don's sister stepped in and gave me the rest. I was so thankful for her kindness.

Before all of this came together, I had prayed and cried out to God, asking Him to help us find a dress, a cake, and a venue. We didn't have the money for extra things like getting my nails done, but once again, God provided. My best friend surprised me by taking me to get my nails done and even bought me some clothes. She capped off the day by taking me out to dinner. I felt so loved and blessed through it all, and I couldn't help but thank God for making a way when I wasn't sure how things would work out.

My family told me they couldn't make it until the 18th, so I decided to move the wedding to June 20th. Don wasn't thrilled about it—he had been set on the original date—but he understood that I really wanted my family there, and that meant the world to me.

Don's mom came through for us again by telling us about a place called the American Legion. They normally charged $300 for a room, but because they loved Don's mom—she was always helping out and cooking amazing meals for people—they gave it to us for only $150. It was such a blessing, and we were incredibly grateful.

With that, we finally had a venue where we could hold both the wedding ceremony and the reception. It felt like everything was falling into place, and I couldn't help but feel that God was providing for us every step of the way.

I never told Don's mom the color of my wedding, but when I saw the cake she arranged, it was the exact color I had chosen. What amazed me even more was that my nieces, without discussing it, dressed their sons in the same color. Everything felt like it was falling into place. My nieces also wore beautiful dresses that perfectly matched the day's vibe. Jamie and Sheena were a tremendous help with the wedding, making the whole experience even more special.

When June 20th, 2014 finally arrived, I was getting ready with my nieces, my auntie, and my little nephew and niece. Out of nowhere, my younger niece, Latrica, surprised me by doing my hair, which was such a blessing. My older niece, Latasha, also gifted me my mama's hat—the same one she used to wear for Easter. When she handed it to me, I broke down in tears. My mom had passed away, and having something of hers on my wedding day made me feel like she was there with me in spirit. It was such a beautiful, emotional moment, and it felt like a piece of her was with me, right there in my heart.

We were all rushing to get ready, and my auntie was waiting for us to finish up. Latrica was finally done with my hair, and just when I thought we were all set, my auntie started getting ready herself. I didn't say anything, but it kind of upset me because we had waited for her, even though I was already finished. Still, the day was coming together beautifully, and I couldn't help but feel grateful for all the love and support surrounding me.

The guests had already started to arrive, and there I was, still needing to finish getting ready. I rushed into the bathroom to put on the final touches. Jamie, our nephew, came in to check on me, asking if I was okay and if I was ready. I had to laugh a little—I wasn't quite there yet. I still needed to put on my dress, but my older niece, Latasha, who was in the wedding, and my auntie were still on their way to the ceremony, giving me a little more time.

By the time I finally made it to the ceremony, it was 4:30 p.m., and I noticed some people had already left. I didn't really understand why, but we kept moving forward with the wedding.

Despite this, everything felt like it was meant to be. Funny enough, a man of God, a prophet from my old church, had once told me to buy a watch because he said I would be late to my own wedding. I didn't believe him at the time, but here I was, and it had come to pass just as he said. Even though things didn't go perfectly, the wedding continued, and I felt such peace knowing that this was the day we had prayed for and worked so hard to make happen.

When Latasha, arrived, we finally began the beautiful ceremony. Don's son was the DJ and played the bridal march, setting the perfect mood. I started my walk down the makeshift aisle between the tables we had set up. As I walked, I carried the beautiful bouquet Don's sister had made for me, feeling so full of happiness. My nephew, Jamie, stood at the end, and Don was right there waiting for me, smiling from ear to ear. The joy on his face made me feel like the most special person in the world.

When I reached Don, Jamie began his speech. I didn't cry, but I was on cloud nine, overflowing with joy. When it was time for the vows, Don and I stood before each other and said, "I do," promising ourselves to one another. Jamie pronounced us husband and wife, and we sealed it with a kiss. Walking hand in hand back down the aisle, everyone clapped and cheered for us—it was such a happy moment.

The reception was filled with dancing and laughter. Don shared a special moment with his mom as they danced together, even though she was in her wheelchair. She was so proud and happy for both of us, and it was heartwarming to see her smile.

We took photos with family and friends, capturing memories that we'll treasure forever. Then, Don and I had our first dance as husband and wife. It was such a beautiful moment—just the two of us, surrounded by the love and support of everyone who had come to celebrate with us.

After the reception, we went back to our apartment, completely exhausted but so incredibly happy. We decided to just go to bed, both of us too wiped out to do anything else. It was a perfect day in every way, and we enjoyed every single second of it.

Chapter 8

In 2017, my father fell ill, and my husband and I drove to Kansas City at the beginning of April to check on him. While we were there, he started to get better. I remember a moment when he was lying in bed, and I was about to feed him with a spoon. I joked, "Here comes the food..." and he burst out laughing. My dad had a very contagious laugh, and I wanted to bring him some joy. As we said our goodbyes, I told him that if he needed anything, I would be there for him, and he smiled.

I recalled how, in 2013, my husband came to Kansas to meet my dad. On that trip, he asked my father for my hand in marriage, and my dad said yes. I remember my dad reassuring him that he wouldn't have to worry about me anymore, and Don promised to take good care of me.

After our visit in early April, my dad felt much better, so we drove back to Denver. But by mid-April, I received a call from one of my siblings saying that Dad's condition had taken a turn for the worse. We learned he had developed pneumonia, his lungs full of fluid. The nurse had informed my siblings that there wasn't much that could be done except keep him comfortable. We drove back to Kansas City to be with him, heading straight to the nursing home.

When we arrived, he tried to talk, but we couldn't understand him. I felt so sad seeing him suffer, and I prayed that God would take him home to end his pain. I could hear the struggle in his breathing, and it broke my heart. I told him that we loved him so much and that Jesus loved him too, encouraging him to be with mom and assuring him we would be okay. Our family gathered that day to spend time with him. We wanted him to feel loved and surrounded.

Eventually, I fell asleep in a recliner next to his bedside. When I woke up the next day, I saw my older nephew nearby, so my husband and I went for breakfast and then returned. As I sat down, I noticed Dad's breathing had become shallower. I realized when he took his last breath that his chest wasn't moving anymore. I got up, moved closer, and put my ear on his chest, but I couldn't hear his heartbeat. I started to cry because I knew he was gone. I informed the nurse and she came in to check him and she confirmed he was gone.

My husband, nephew, and I cried as we called the family to tell them that Dad had passed away at 11:21 AM on April 21st, 2017. A week later, we buried him. While it was incredibly sad, I felt relieved that he was no longer suffering. I wasn't angry with God; I understood that it was better for him to go, and now he was free from pain. Yes, I was sad, but I also felt a sense of peace knowing he was finally at rest.

Chapter 9

I was working at a nursing facility and ended up staying there for almost six years. However, I started to feel tired of the job and began looking for something new. I went to several interviews, but I kept getting rejected. They would compliment my personality and my resume, but they all said I needed more experience. It was frustrating, and I found myself praying for guidance from God.

Finally, I decided to put in my two weeks' notice, feeling ready to move on. But when I did, my job didn't want me to leave. They offered me a great raise, and in the end, I decided to stay. It was a moment of realization that sometimes what we think we want isn't what's best for us.

Around that time, my good friend, Mrs. Dorris, told me something that hit home. She said, "Stop running from God." I hadn't realized it, but she was right—I was running from His will for my life. I heard her words but didn't act on them immediately.

Then, in January 2020, I began hearing about this deadly virus. At first, they didn't know where it came from, but it was spreading fast. By March, everything changed. Our facility went into lockdown, and it became difficult for family members to visit residents. We were required to wear masks, hospital gowns, and gloves constantly. The fear of the unknown gripped everyone.

One day, I started feeling unusually hot and thirsty. I drank water like crazy, running to the bathroom every 15 minutes. A nurse told me to get checked out because it sounded like diabetes. Around the same time, we received new machines to measure blood pressure and pulse ox. When they tested mine, my blood pressure was extremely high, and everyone was concerned. They urged me to see a doctor, but I didn't have health insurance and didn't want to rack up a huge hospital bill. I went to a clinic, but when they wanted to run more tests, I decided to hold off.

By April 5th, 2020, I felt completely drained. I was a CNA and still worked hard, even though I was struggling. On my lunch break, all suited up in our protective gear, I passed by my boss. She took one look at me and asked if I wanted to go home because I didn't look well. I wanted to finish my tasks, so I pushed through, even though I felt like I could collapse any moment.

After finishing up, I called my husband to come get me. When I clocked out and got into the car, the sickness hit me even harder. By the time we reached home, I could barely move. We lived on the third floor, and it took me 20-30 minutes just to climb the stairs. I kept having to sit down to rest.

When I finally made it inside, I was so weak. I took off all my clothes and collapsed on the bed. I couldn't stop throwing up, and I kept rushing to the bathroom. I was so thirsty that I ate a bunch of oranges, but nothing seemed to help.

Monday morning came, and I was still incredibly sick. My job called to check on me, and I told them how awful I felt. They wished me well and said they were thinking of me. By Tuesday, nothing had changed. I was still throwing up and couldn't move. My job called again, and I vaguely remember talking to them, but after that, everything became a blur.

The next thing I remember, I was struggling to even get up to use the bathroom. I was lying in bed, barely conscious, and then suddenly, I recall the fire department being in my apartment. Everything felt surreal, like a blur, as if I was in a movie. I vaguely remember them moving me, seeing the light from the ceiling shift as they carried me. Faces were around me, but they were just shapes—I couldn't make out any details. I was in and out of consciousness.

Apparently, my husband had asked if he should call 911, and I told him yes, though I don't even remember saying that. I don't remember being put in the car or even arriving at the hospital. It was a Friday, and the next clear memory I have is waking up in the hospital, throwing up. A sweet nurse and a CNA were there, cleaning me up as I drifted in and out of awareness. I remember feeling awful for making such a mess and apologizing to them, but they were so kind and understanding, reassuring me as they helped me sit up so I wouldn't throw up on myself.

There was another moment when a nurse gently gave me a bed bath. Her kindness and patience touched me deeply, even though I was barely able to stay awake. My poor husband was so worried about me, but because of COVID, he wasn't allowed to visit. No one was. Even though he was desperate to be by my side, the restrictions kept us apart. It broke my heart to think of him, worrying alone, unable to see me or know how I was doing.

The whole experience was a fog of pain, fear, and flashes of kindness from the hospital staff. Through it all, I could feel the weight of everything—my own helplessness, my husband's anxiety, and the uncertainty of what would happen next. But I was grateful for those moments of care, those people who made me feel human when I felt so fragile.

One nurse gave me her cell phone so I could talk to my husband, but I don't even remember what we talked about. It was such a kind gesture, though, one that stood out even amidst all the confusion. After that, I was out again.

When I finally came to, I learned I had been in the ICU for three days, in and out of a diabetic coma. My blood sugar had skyrocketed to 823, dangerously high. The doctor later told my husband that if he had waited any longer to call 911, I would have slipped into a full coma, and there was no telling how long I would have been in it—or worse, I could have died.

While I was lying in that ICU bed, everything around me felt so quiet and peaceful. In the stillness, I could feel God's presence with me. He spoke to my heart, telling me to forgive my husband and to let go of the past. At first, I hesitated. I thought for a moment that maybe God was getting ready to take me home with Him. But then, I caught myself—what was I doing? I repented and asked God for forgiveness, and in that moment, He gave me peace.

Not long after, two ladies from physical therapy came into the room to help me stand. They set me up on the edge of the bed and asked if I could stand up. I couldn't at first, so they helped me to my feet. Then they asked if I could stand on my own, and I said yes. As I stood there, I thanked Jesus. The two ladies were laughing and thanking Jesus right along with me. I stood for a few minutes, and they didn't want me to get too tired, so they had me sit back down on the bed. I laid down to rest.

I don't know what day it was exactly, but I remember waking up to the sound of rain falling outside the window. The sound was so soothing, like a lullaby from nature. The nurse came in and tried to turn on the TV for me, but I asked him not to. I just wanted to soak in the peaceful quiet.

It's funny, when I was younger, I couldn't stand being alone or having things too quiet. Now, it feels like a blessing. It's crazy how much life changes you, how things that once felt unbearable can become the very things you long for.

When the doctors told me I was well enough to leave the ICU, they released me and moved me upstairs. There was so much that happened during my time in the ICU. One of the things they wanted to see was if I could feed myself. It was a struggle, but I did it, even though it took me a long time. I was so weak. I even tried to eat some ice cream, which I love, but it took me forever to finish it.

Fast forward to when I was upstairs recovering, I had a strange dream. In the dream, my husband came to get me out of the hospital. I was wearing a short outfit, and he was driving this old turquoise blue truck. We were heading back to Kansas City to my old church. When we arrived at the church, everyone there looked like fishes from the movie *Finding Nemo*—bright blue and yellow fish. It was such a vivid dream, and though I didn't fully understand it, it stayed with me.

When I was finally released from the hospital, I couldn't have been happier. The CNAs, nurses, and doctors had been so wonderful to me, and I felt incredibly grateful for the care I received at Swedish Hospital. The people who brought me my meals, the nurses who checked on me, and the CNAs who encouraged me were all so kind. I wanted to thank every single one of them—I will never forget how they took care of me.

The day my husband came to pick me up, he was so excited. He kissed me, hugged me, and just held me, happy to have me out of the hospital. I was still very weak, but we gathered my things, including my machine to check my blood sugar, and headed home. When we got to our apartment, I looked at the stairs and dreaded them. It was so difficult, and it took me about 30 minutes to make it up, stopping several times along the way. But I made it, and when I finally reached the bedroom, I was thankful for the adjustable bed we had invested in—it helped so much with my recovery.

I was exhausted, but there was a moment that really broke me. I was trying to open the package for my machine to check my blood sugar, and my hands were too weak to do it. I felt so frustrated and defeated. I started crying, my mind clouded with emotions, and I think I cried myself to sleep. But before I drifted off, I had managed to open the package.

When I woke up, that strange dream I had in the hospital came back to me, and I couldn't shake the feeling that it meant something. As I was pondering it, God spoke to me. He told me that He wanted me to return to my first love and to do the work He had called me to when He first saved me. He was calling me back to His will, and in that moment, I knew I had to listen.

Part 3

We Should Always Plant Seeds

Chapter 10

After my son's funeral, I started attending Praise Chapel. It became a blessing in my walk with Christ, allowing me to learn more about Jesus and deepening my relationship with Him. God placed some wonderful people in my life through this church. They truly believed in the Word of God, and the leaders lived it out daily.

We participated in outreach efforts in the community to reach the lost, and it was an amazing experience. This is where I learned how to serve and witness to others. I would always ask God what I should say, and I had the privilege of being surrounded by amazing people who were skilled at winning souls.

One person, in particular, became a close friend of mine. She had a beautiful relationship with Jesus and was incredibly talented at rapping and singing for Him. What I admired most about her was how easily she related to others and connected with everyone around her.

Being part of this incredible church taught me how to witness to people about Jesus. We would go to the west part of town, where many people were out partying. I remember one instance when I saw a lady waiting with her friends at a crosswalk, clearly drunk. While her friends started walking and left her behind, the Lord led me to tell her that Jesus would never leave her behind. She looked at me and smiled slightly. I was about to say more, but one of her friends returned to take her away. Still, I knew a seed had been sown.

On another occasion, a Muslim man approached me to talk about Jesus. I told him that Jesus loved him, and he began to share his beliefs about Allah. I asked Jesus what I should say next. I can't recall the exact words He gave me, but I remember that when I spoke them, the man fell silent. After a long pause, he said it made sense to him. I knew then that another seed had been planted.

There was another time when we witnessed to and prayed with people, seeing God touch their hearts. It was incredible to be part of God's Kingdom and witness how He moved. We reached out to the poor by giving food, blankets, and coats. I felt truly blessed to be part of the team.

―――

"And they overcame him by the blood of the Lamb and by the word of their testimony, and they did not love their lives to the death." Revelation 12:11

Acknowledgment

I want to take a moment to acknowledge P, my editor, publisher, and a wonderful friend that God has blessed me with. She has helped me tremendously throughout this journey, and I am truly grateful for her support. There have been many others who have also played a significant role in this process. They know who they are, and I want to thank all of them for believing in me and encouraging me to pursue this dream. Your faith in me has made a world of difference, and I couldn't have done it without you.

About the Author

Born and raised in Kansas City, I am the youngest of four siblings, with one older sister and two older brothers. I now live in Denver with my husband, where I am actively involved in my church community. Serving others and giving back has always been a joy for me, and my faith continues to shape the way I live and serve.

www.ingramcontent.com/pod-product-compliance
Lightning Source LLC
Chambersburg PA
CBHW01202305O526
44107CB00102B/716